THINGS ON WHEELS

Kate Little

Designed by Steve Page

Illustrated by Peter Bull

Contents

629.1 [T]

Going places on wheels

This book is all about different types of things on wheels. It shows what the very first bicycles, motorbikes, cars and trains looked like and explains how they work. You can also find out about different types of racing vehicles.

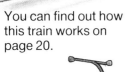

You can find out how this train works on page 20.

These are the working parts of a car. You can find out how they work on pages 6 to 9.

On page 16 you can see the differences between an old-fashioned high-wheeled bicycle and a modern bicycle.

The very first motorbike was made of wood. On page 17 you can see how much they have changed.

This is a Formula 1 racing car. Find out about other motor sports on page 12.

The wheel story

Before wheels were invented, tree trunks were used as rollers to help push heavy loads along the ground.

The first wheels were made of solid wood about 6,000 years ago. Later, they were fixed to carts pulled by horses and oxen.

Then wheels were made with wooden spokes, which made them lighter. An iron rim round the edge made them last longer.

What makes them go ?

Person power

The first bicycle had no pedals. It only went as fast as the rider could push it along with his feet.

Steam engines

Steam trains burned coal or wood. The fire heated a tank of water. Steam from this pushed a rod which made the wheels turn round.

Petrol power

The engine in a car and a motorbike is called the internal combustion engine. It burns petrol inside it to make the wheels turn.

The first four-wheeled car was a horse-drawn carriage with an engine fitted to it. It was built in 1886 by a German called Gottlieb Daimler.

Later, wheels were made with metal spokes. They were much stronger and lighter, so were good for bicycle wheels.

Train wheels are made of very strong steel. They have a ridge on the inside to stop them running off the track.

All car and bicycle wheels have air filled (pneumatic) tyres. These make riding over bumps in the road more comfortable.

Parts of the car

In a car factory, all the pieces needed to make a car are arranged in order. As each car moves along a line, all the parts are fitted to it. This is called an assembly line. At the end the car is finished and needs to be tested for any faults.

These strong steel bars lower the car body down on to the chassis.

The chassis

The engine, clutch and gearbox, driveshaft, rear axle, rear differential and suspension are all supported in a steel frame called the chassis. (This has been left out of the picture to make it clearer).

The engine is cased in and fitted to the front of the car.

The driveshaft joins the engine and gearbox to the rear axle.

Engine

Gearstick

Gearbox

Bumper

Radiator

The clutch and the gearbox allow the car to be driven at different speeds and to go backwards.

Clutch

Lights

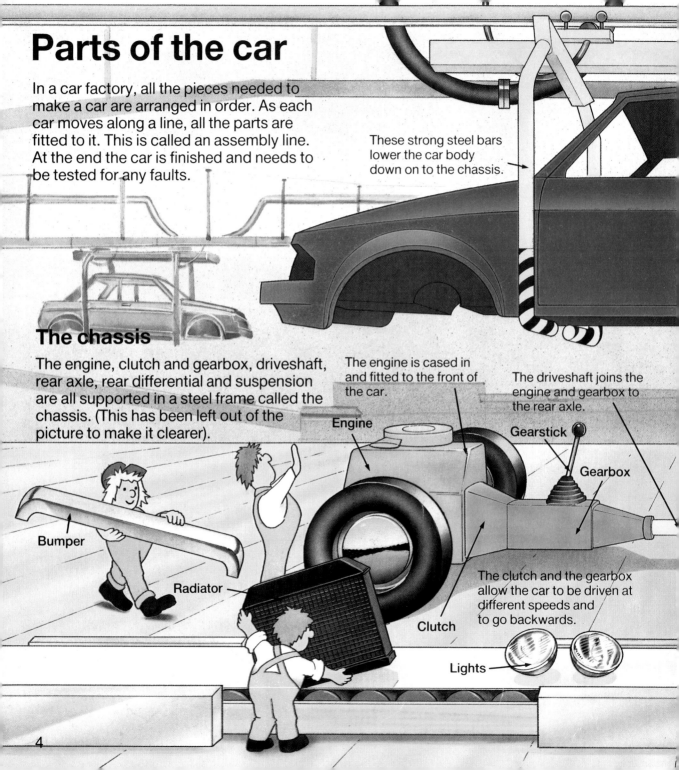

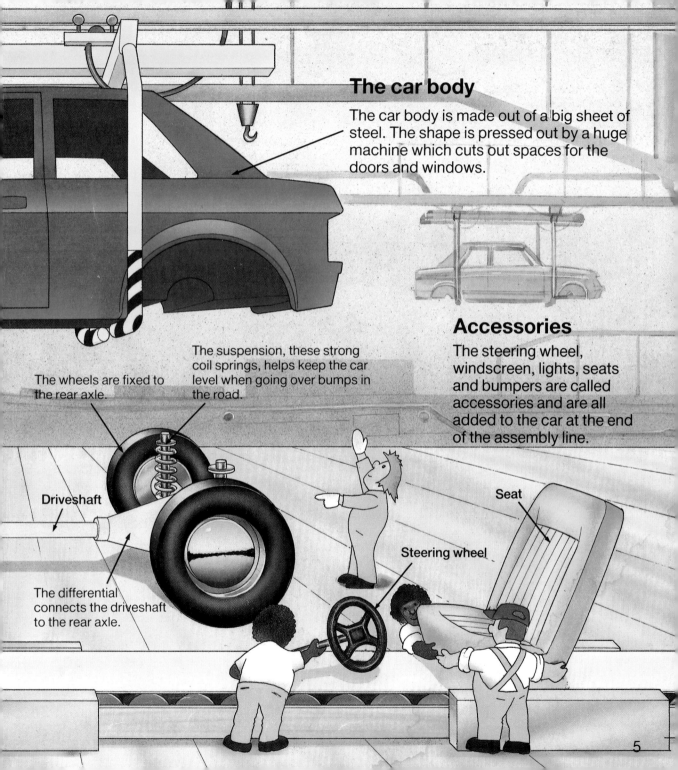

The car body

The car body is made out of a big sheet of steel. The shape is pressed out by a huge machine which cuts out spaces for the doors and windows.

Accessories

The steering wheel, windscreen, lights, seats and bumpers are called accessories and are all added to the car at the end of the assembly line.

The suspension, these strong coil springs, helps keep the car level when going over bumps in the road.

The wheels are fixed to the rear axle.

Driveshaft

The differential connects the driveshaft to the rear axle.

Seat

Steering wheel

5

How an engine works

A car engine has many different moving parts that need to be kept oiled to keep it working well. Car engines run on a mixture of petrol and air which burns explosively inside the engine.

When the engine is switched on, the pistons move up and down inside the cylinders. This up and down movement turns the crankshaft round. The crankshaft turns the driveshaft, which makes the wheels go round.

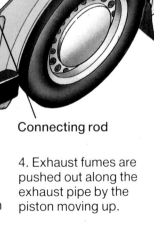

Spark plug

Cylinder

Piston

Carburettor

Radiator

The carburettor

Petrol is mixed with air in the carburettor before it goes into the cylinder.

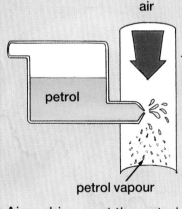

air

petrol

petrol vapour

Air rushing past the petrol breaks it up into tiny droplets so small you cannot see them. This is called petrol vapour.

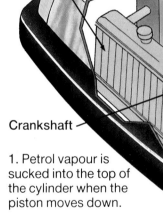

Crankshaft

1. Petrol vapour is sucked into the top of the cylinder when the piston moves down.

2. The piston moves up and squeezes the petrol vapour into a small space in the top of the cylinder.

3. An electric spark from the spark plug sets light to the petrol vapour. It explodes, pushing the piston down.

Connecting rod

4. Exhaust fumes are pushed out along the exhaust pipe by the piston moving up.

6

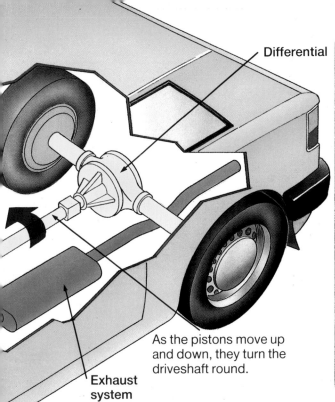

Differential

As the pistons move up and down, they turn the driveshaft round.

Exhaust system

This engine has four cylinders. More powerful engines have as many as six or 12 cylinders.

Driving the rear wheels ★

At the end of the driveshaft is a cogged wheel or gear which connects to a larger gear on the rear axle.

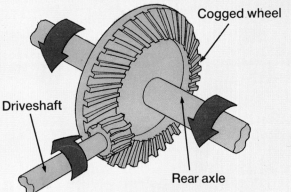

Cogged wheel

Driveshaft

Rear axle

The teeth of one gear fit into the other to make it turn. This makes the power from the engine drive the rear axle and rear wheels.

Piston power

The force that fires a cannonball from a cannon is similar to the force which pushes the pistons in the cylinders. When the gunpowder is lit, it explodes and hot gases force the ball out.

Hot engines

The radiator is a narrow metal box which contains water. Water is pumped around the engine to keep it cool.

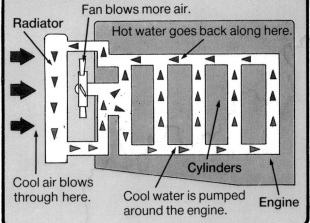

Fan blows more air.

Radiator

Hot water goes back along here.

Cool air blows through here.

Cool water is pumped around the engine.

Cylinders

Engine

★This picture is simplified. There are actually many more gear wheels in this part, (the "differential") to allow the rear wheels to go at different speeds round corners.

On the road

On these pages you can find out how the clutch and gears make the car go at different speeds and how the brakes work.

What are gears?

Gears are cogged wheels which fit together and turn at different speeds depending on the number of teeth they have.

This gear has 10 teeth.

This gear has 20 teeth.

Gear stick

The small one turns twice as fast as the big one.

Gearbox

Brake pedal

Most cars have four forward gears and one reverse. Trucks can have as many as 16 gears.

How the gearbox works

The top row of gears inside the gearbox are turned by the engine. They turn the bottom row, which make the wheels go round.

Most cars have drum brakes on rear wheels.

Using the gears

When starting off, the driver puts the engine into first gear. It needs a lot of power to get the car moving.

Second and third gear help the car to gain speed.

Fourth gear is used for driving along at a fast, steady speed.

Reverse gear changes the direction of the wheels so the car goes backwards.

How the clutch works

To change gear the driver has to press the clutch pedal down. This separates the two discs and stops the engine from turning the wheels.

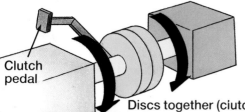

Clutch pedal

Discs together (clutch engaged)

Discs apart (clutch disengaged)

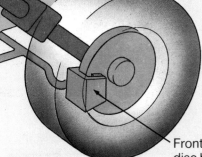

Front brakes are usually disc brakes.

Steering a car

Steering is worked by gears too. Instead of two cogged wheels there is a rack and a pinion.

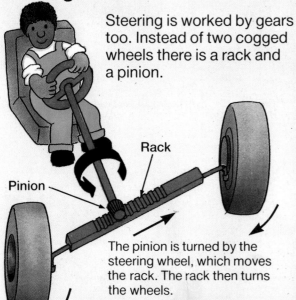

Rack

Pinion

The pinion is turned by the steering wheel, which moves the rack. The rack then turns the wheels.

How the brakes work

When the driver presses the brake pedal, pads are forced to rub against all four wheels. When they rub together, a force called friction stops them moving. Friction between the brakes and the wheels makes a car slow down.

Drum brakes

The brake drum is fixed inside the wheel. So when the brake shoes press out against the drum, the wheels slow down and stop.

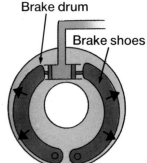

Brake drum

Brake shoes

Disc brakes

A steel disc is fixed inside the wheel. When the brake pads press in on the disc, friction stops the wheel moving.

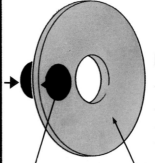

Brake pads   **Steel disc**

Grand Prix racing

Winning the Grand Prix Championship is the greatest achievement of all motor racing. Drivers and cars battle for ten months of the year on race tracks all over the world. They cover 5,470km (3,400 miles) during the 16 Grand Prix races. The drivers score points if they are among the first six to finish each race. There are two world championships, one for the cars and one for the drivers.

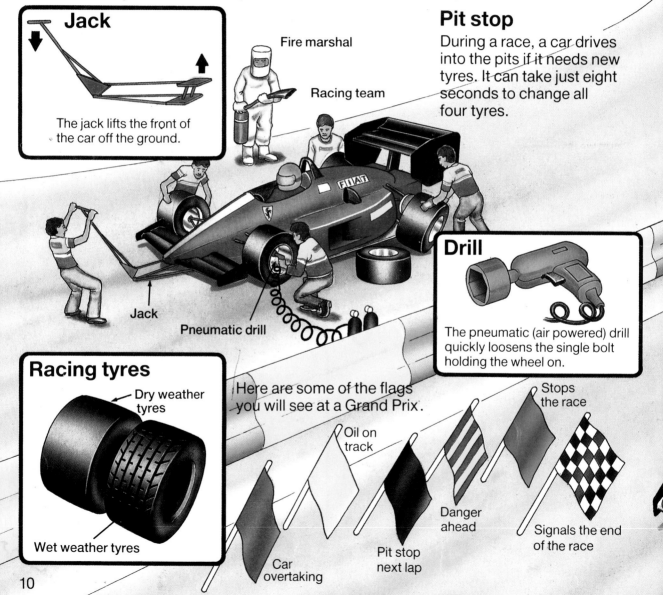

Jack

The jack lifts the front of the car off the ground.

Fire marshal

Racing team

Pit stop

During a race, a car drives into the pits if it needs new tyres. It can take just eight seconds to change all four tyres.

Jack

Pneumatic drill

Drill

The pneumatic (air powered) drill quickly loosens the single bolt holding the wheel on.

Racing tyres

Dry weather tyres

Wet weather tyres

Here are some of the flags you will see at a Grand Prix.

Oil on track

Stops the race

Danger ahead

Car overtaking

Pit stop next lap

Signals the end of the race

Driving seat

The driver's seat is moulded exactly to his shape.

The engine is so powerful it uses 4.5 litres (1 gallon) of petrol every 8km (5 miles). The cheapest Formula 1 engine costs as much as six family saloon cars.

Air pushes down on the aerofoils at the front and back to keep the car on the ground.

Air pushes down here

The driver has a radio fitted inside his helmet so he can talk to his team during the race.

Aerofoil

The car is only 76cm (30 inches) high. It cuts through the air easily because it is so long and low.

Brake duct

Safety

The driver wears a fireproof hood under his helmet to protect his face.

Different styles of racing helmets.

Petrol is carried in rubberized tanks all around the driver.

The rear tyres are nearly 48cm (19 inches) wide. They are smooth and sticky to touch, and grip the track well. The driver can race round corners at up to 152km/h (95mph).

The brakes can slow the car from 290 to 65km/h (180 to 40mph) in under three seconds. As they get very hot during a race, these ducts let air blow on to the brakes to cool them down.

11

Motor sports

There are many types of motor sports. Here are just three of them. The cars are all different and have been specially prepared in some way for their particular sport.

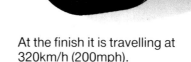

Aerofoil

Drag racing

Drag racing is a test of speed between two dragster cars. They race on a straight track over 400m (1/4 of a mile).

Slicks

A drag race

The driver makes the rear tyres spin round. This makes them hot and sticky so the car gets a good grip on the track when starting.

In just two seconds the car accelerates from 0 to 160km/h (0 to 100mph).

At the finish it is travelling at 320km/h (200mph).

Parachutes help slow the car down.

Start

Finish

Stock car racing

In stock car racing, old cars are raced on oval shaped dirt tracks.

Different classes of races are held for different types of cars.

All windows and back seats are taken out for safety.

Powerful brakes, suspension and engine are fitted.

Safety

Roll bar

Safety harness

Safety harness and roll bar protect the driver if the car turns over.

Slingshot dragster

The rear tyres, called slicks, have no tread and are made of very soft rubber. The front wheels are very light and thin, like bicycle wheels.

The high aerofoil at the back and the one between the front wheels stop the car lifting off the ground.

Aerofoil

Funny cars

This dragster is called a Funny Car. It has a top speed of 418km/h (260mph). To make the car go fast it burns rocket fuel in its engine.

This old Ford Anglia has been fitted with a special engine and fat rear tyres to race in a mixed class.

Rallying

Rallies are held on snowy mountain roads, across rough country and through deserts all over the world.

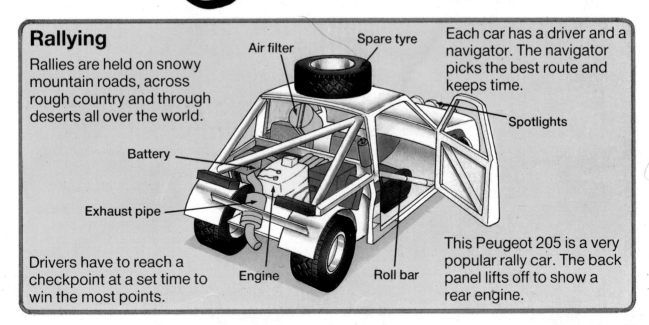

Air filter

Spare tyre

Each car has a driver and a navigator. The navigator picks the best route and keeps time.

Spotlights

Battery

Exhaust pipe

Engine

Roll bar

Drivers have to reach a checkpoint at a set time to win the most points.

This Peugeot 205 is a very popular rally car. The back panel lifts off to show a rear engine.

Off the road

Some cars are specially designed to travel over very rugged ground where there are no roads. An ordinary car is designed to run on good roads and would soon break down in conditions like these. The exhaust pipe would be knocked off, the tyres would burst and it could not go through rivers.

'County' Station Wagon

The Land Rover was designed for driving in rough country. This one looks very much like the first Land Rover ever built in 1948. The design has not changed much because it is so good.

The car body is high off the ground. It is bolted together in sections, so it will not bend or twist.

Spare tyre

Front axle

Front differential

Rear axle

Folding side step

Tough aluminium body

Rear differential

Extra springy suspension cushions the driver and passengers from bumps.

Big, chunky tyres help the car grip uneven ground. They are made with very thick rubber so they will not split.

What is four wheel drive?

An ordinary car has one differential which drives either the front or the rear wheels. A four wheel drive car has a differential at the front and the back so the engine turns all four wheels. This means that four wheel drive vehicles travel well over mud, snow or sand.

Rear axle

Engine

Driveshaft

Rear differential

Front axle

Front differential

What can four wheel drive do?

These are some of the things that four wheel drive (4WD) cars can do.

This Land Rover can be driven through rivers up to 50cm (20in) deep.

This pick-up truck can climb very steep slopes because of the extra power in its wheels.

This jeep can be driven on steeply banked tracks without it tipping over.

Tyres

Heavy duty tyres with deep tread for going over rocks and sand.

Other 4WD vehicles

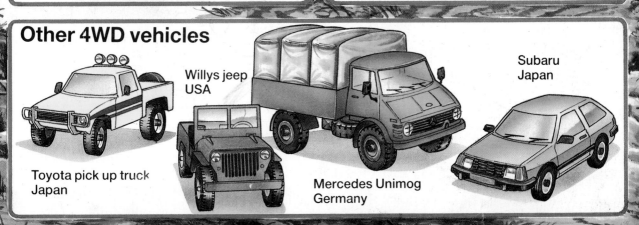

Toyota pick up truck
Japan

Willys jeep
USA

Mercedes Unimog
Germany

Subaru
Japan

Bicycles

The first bicycle, called a hobbyhorse, was built about 150 years ago. It had a front wheel that could be turned but no pedals. Later, pedals were fixed to the front wheel to make the bicycle go faster.

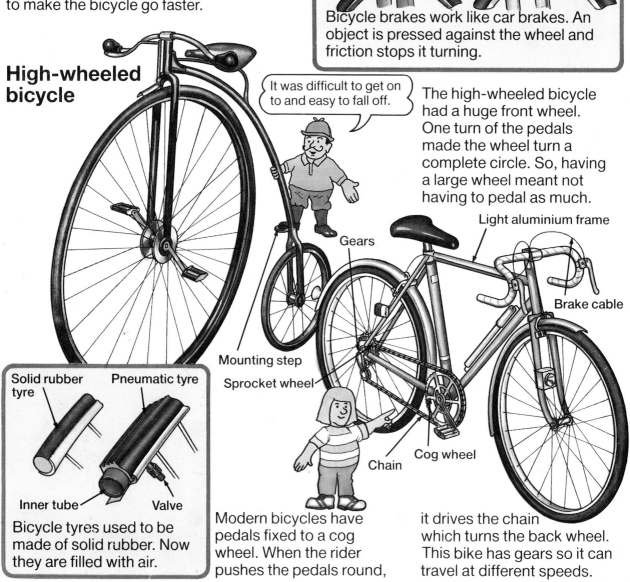

Spoon brake

Brake block

Bicycle brakes work like car brakes. An object is pressed against the wheel and friction stops it turning.

High-wheeled bicycle

It was difficult to get on to and easy to fall off.

The high-wheeled bicycle had a huge front wheel. One turn of the pedals made the wheel turn a complete circle. So, having a large wheel meant not having to pedal as much.

Light aluminium frame

Gears

Brake cable

Mounting step

Sprocket wheel

Cog wheel

Chain

Solid rubber tyre

Pneumatic tyre

Inner tube

Valve

Bicycle tyres used to be made of solid rubber. Now they are filled with air.

Modern bicycles have pedals fixed to a cog wheel. When the rider pushes the pedals round,

it drives the chain which turns the back wheel. This bike has gears so it can travel at different speeds.

Motorbikes

The first motorbike was built about 120 years ago. It was a bicycle fitted with a steam engine. Now there are many different types of motorbike for different racing sports.

Road racing

A Grand Prix racing bike is the fastest bike built today. The engine is covered in so the bike can cut through the air.

Arrows show the movement of air over the bike.

The rider crouches forward so the wind rushes over him.

Sidecar racing

Low, streamlined shape

During a race, the passenger leans right out of the sidecar to balance it as it speeds round corners.

Trials bikes

Strong suspension

Trials riding is a cross-country competition which tests the skill of the rider. The bike has strong tyres to help it grip over rocks and through mud.

Dragbikes

Wide rear tyres (slicks).

Dragbikes have very powerful engines. The rider lies right across the bike so it travels faster through the wind.

Types of trains

The first railway tracks were built about 400 years ago, when animals were used to pull heavy loads along rails. At that time, the rails were made of wood.

The very first engines were driven by steam. Today trains are pulled by diesel engines and electric motors. On these pages you can see all three types.

Steam trains

American type 4-4-0

The American type 4-4-0 was one of the first steam trains to cross America.

The smokestack catches sparks from the fire.

Bell

Boiler

The tender carries wood for the fire.

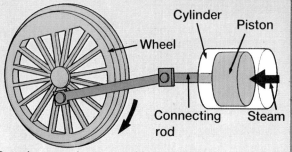

How steam turns the wheels

Wheel

Cylinder

Piston

Connecting rod

Steam

Burning coal or wood heats water in a large tank, called a boiler. Steam from the boiling water pushes pistons in a cylinder. The pistons are connected to the wheels.

Driving wheels power the train.

Leading wheels guide the train around bends.

Cowcatcher to push stray animals off the track.

Electric trains

Electric trains are the fastest in the world. They pick up electricity from overhead cables or from a third track on the ground.

Hikari express

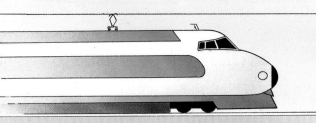

This Japanese train, nicknamed 'The Bullet' can travel at 209km/h (130mph).

Diesel trains

British Rail Inter-City 125

This train has a diesel engine. It is the same as a car engine but burns diesel oil instead of petrol. The diesel engine produces electricity in a generator. Electricity goes along cables to motors which turn the wheels and work the heaters and lights.

Underground railways

The guide wheels keep the train on the tracks.

Steel beam

On the Metro, the Paris underground, the trains run on pneumatic tyres. The trains are faster and quieter with rubber wheels.

The bogie

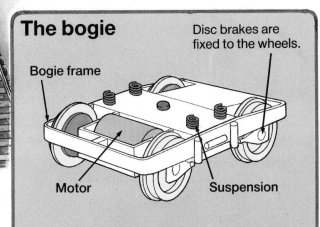

Disc brakes are fixed to the wheels.

Bogie frame

Motor

Suspension

The train carriages rest on top of bogies like this one. It lets the train bend as it goes around corners.

Trains today

Today's high speed trains are built for fast inter-city travel. This French TGV (Train à Grande Vitesse which means 'high speed train') has an average speed of 260km/h (161mph), which makes it the fastest passenger train in the world. A special track was built for it, without sharp bends and steep hills.

There are no signals on the TGV track for the driver to look for. Instead, electronic signals are sent to the driver's cab. They tell the driver what speed to travel.

The driver has a radio-telephone in the cab and there are emergency telephones beside the track every 1km (0.6 miles).

There is a locomotive carriage at each end of the train. This is what powers the train.

Driver's cab

Concrete sleepers

SNCF

Tracks

Steel rail

Electric motors here turn the wheels.

SNCF

The distance between the two parallel tracks of a railway line is called the gauge. Throughout the world there is a standard gauge which is 1.43m (4ft 8½ inches).

The track is raised on one side so that the train can speed round corners.

20

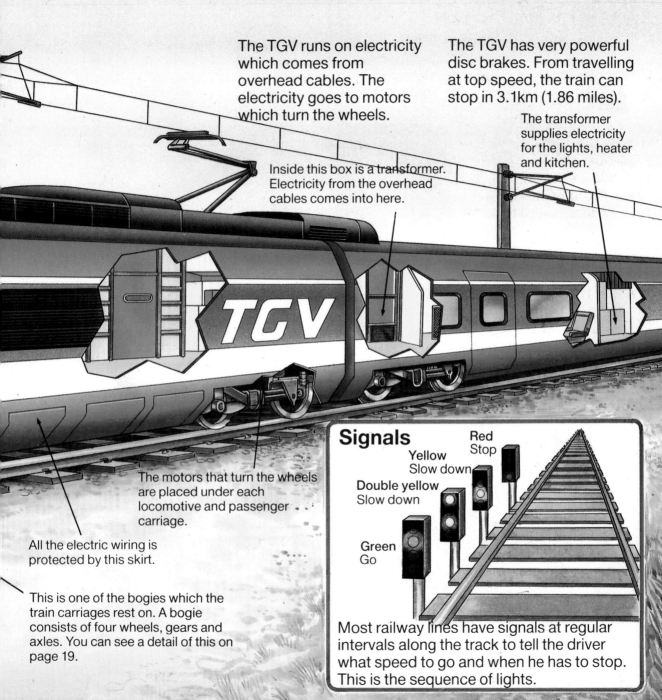

The TGV runs on electricity which comes from overhead cables. The electricity goes to motors which turn the wheels.

The TGV has very powerful disc brakes. From travelling at top speed, the train can stop in 3.1km (1.86 miles).

The transformer supplies electricity for the lights, heater and kitchen.

Inside this box is a transformer. Electricity from the overhead cables comes into here.

The motors that turn the wheels are placed under each locomotive and passenger carriage.

All the electric wiring is protected by this skirt.

This is one of the bogies which the train carriages rest on. A bogie consists of four wheels, gears and axles. You can see a detail of this on page 19.

Signals

Red
Stop

Yellow
Slow down

Double yellow
Slow down

Green
Go

Most railway lines have signals at regular intervals along the track to tell the driver what speed to go and when he has to stop. This is the sequence of lights.

21

Fastest on wheels

The first cars and motorbikes travelled very slowly. A hundred years ago, cars in Britain were only allowed to go at 6.4km/h (4mph). A man had to walk in front of the car to make sure the driver kept within the speed limit.

Fastest on the road

Aston Martin V8 Vantage

The Aston Martin V8 Vantage is one of the world's fastest and most powerful cars. It can accelerate from 0 to 161km/h (0 to 100mph) in just 11.9 seconds.

It has a top speed of 270km/h (168mph).

Car factories, like British Leyland, produce one car every six minutes. An Aston Martin takes 16 weeks to produce because each car is hand-built.

Fastest on rails

These trains are the fastest steam, diesel and electric trains in the world. They have all set speed records in the past and have been responsible for cutting down journey times between main cities. Here you can see how far each could travel in one hour.

Flying Scotsman (UK)

LNER Mallard (UK)

96km (60 miles)

161km (100 miles)

The Flying Scotsman was the first steam locomotive to provide a non-stop service from London to Edinburgh.

In 1938, Mallard set a new record for steam engines, travelling at 203km/h (126mph). No other steam train has travelled faster.

Kawasaki GPZ1000RX

The fastest motorbike on the road today is the Kawasaki GPZ1000. It can travel at over 260km/h (161mph).

The rider is protected from the wind by sleek panels. Holes in each side panel let cool air blow on to the engine to stop it from overheating.

World Land Speed Record

This is a test of speed run over a straight mile (1.6km). The vehicles competing must make one run in each direction within an hour.

Car class

Thrust 2, broke the speed record in 1983. The car travelled at an average speed of 1,019.4km/h (633.45mph).

Motorbike class

This very unusual motorbike, Lightning Bolt, broke the speed record in 1978, travelling at an average speed of 512.7km/h (318.59mph).

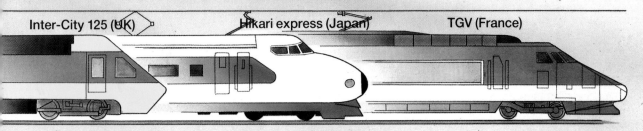

Inter-City 125 (UK)   Hikari express (Japan)   TGV (France)

200km (125miles)   210km (130miles)   260km (161 miles)

The Inter-City 125 is the fastest diesel train in the world. It can reach a top speed of 231km/h (143mph).

Japanese National Railways built a new track for this train which speeds along at over 210km/h (130mph).

This is the fastest train in the world. During tests it reached an amazing top speed of 390km/h (236mph).

23

Index

First published in 1987 by
Usborne Publishing Ltd,
20 Garrick Street,
London WC2E 9BJ,
England.

© 1987 Usborne Publishing Ltd.

The name Usborne and the device 🐝 are the Trade Marks of Usborne Publishing Ltd.

Printed in Belgium.